Touched:

Grief and Loss

Poetry & Impressions

JLR Spear

Table of Contents

Preface

Thank you for investing your time and precious funds to read this book. Welcome, sit back and grab a cup of tea, coffee, glass of wine. Merely suggestions, to join nature or perhaps draw a hot bath and soak as you read. May the words inspire you, elevate you, help you feel loved, held, and understood. These poems are a culmination of various individual's experiences during grief and loss, written in poetic form through one writer. Raw, real, imperfect, and heartfelt. Passionate observations, insights, revelations, and just sheer emotions during most difficult times shared, vulnerably. Many of us would like to wish out of existence the horrible moments experienced right after loss. Some choose to hide and conceal grief. These entries are the creative culmination of all such experiences into one style and basic form to share with many, as several individuals have contributed to these works. It is advised you do not expect perfection. Rather, imperfection, which does exist within these pages just as in human reality.

The guttural cries to understand grief and loss within the human experience are furthest from perfection, yet blessed and necessary. Introspective journeys shared here of individuals surviving tragedies of heinous unsolved murders, loss of closest friends and relatives. It is a real view, solemn yet hopeful at times. Discouraging and encouraging, confusion, clarity, unique...yet common to us all during extremely trying times. It is the hope of JLR Spear, you resonate with the emotions, plights, struggles, and triumphs of the works here, representing many including the writer, a part of JLR Spear. May you cry, laugh, and be pricked to dig a bit deeper to find hidden jewels within the prose and yourself... finding the courage to persevere. Empowering yourself and others or just simply enjoy and feel the rhythms, cues, infiltrating the creativity of others and JLR Spear. There is light dropped in here and there as to not allow the writings to become too heavy. That light is continued within the pages of the next book in the series, Segway if you will, into Touched: From Beyond. These individuals continue to share their journeys with you into strange, new happenings and experiences of the supernatural kind. Even if you choose not to acquire a copy of the second book due to beliefs, etc... It is hoped that you receive comfort from this book alone.

There is something here for almost everyone, past, present, future...written in truth of the feel of grief and loss.

Disclaimer: this book is not recommended for Ph.D.'s and critics. I am proud to say you will find nothing but rubbish within these pages, most likely believing works to be unworthy of even printing or publishing. I am thankful, as it is not for that population, to which their opinions mean nothing in this regard. These poems are for the everyday common people of all colors, creeds, genders, ages, identities. For the budding writer and artist, those hurt and healing, those with a Master degree, BS, AS, trade school, medical license, or little to some education. Welcome! This is for you!

You are those I wish to reach, caress with words, appeal to, and share these poems with.

Ph.D.'s may wish to go ahead and exit or return the book. No hard feelings. If you happen to have a Ph.D. and enjoy the work, my apologies, you are very rare!

To the rest of you, thank you for taking the journey with JLR Spear into Touched: Grief and Loss.

Stay tuned to the upcoming Touched: From Beyond by JLR Spear also to be released in 2021. Blessings...enjoy!

JLR Spear

Acknowledgment

Thank you to all the lives lived on Earth; especially the kind past over, present, and future remaining with us, the living. Those lost mean something to someone. Never forgotten, never gone...embodied and carried on through us all. Your lives are honored, your spirit appreciated more than the living can communicate. Rest peacefully, your cause and your essence endure. I honor you all with such gratitude for who you were, who you are to us, and who you will continue to be to those who love you, eternally.

Thank you to all of you current souls that have been through the absolute worst experiences and survived to tell the tales. Thank you for sharing your stories, encouraging others to do the same. To all of those that have suffered through divorce, letting go, loss of a parent, losing a child, suicide, terror of war, frontline workers seeing death daily and persevering through it all...Thank you for pushing through.

"All heartache is heartache ...equally tragic and relevant to the one whom experiences it"...JLR Spear.

Thank you to all individuals expressing themselves through catharsis in tragedy as well as the pleasant times...please keep creating. Encouragement for those in throws of tragedy right now, God be with you. Hold on, it will get better. This book and the rest coming in the series are for all of you, in honor of you.

A Castle; Soul

Breaching the castle gates,
Threshold broken...
Unwanted intruder!
Security compromised,
On alert!
Screams heard,
Pillagers! Looters!

Shock wanes,
Then come feelings of grief,
Unexpected;
Loss of a previously known life...
Shattered substance,
The knowing of safety...
Turned upon the edge of a knife.

Just as it will take months,
Years to repair the castle torn.
So it will take that long,

For the soul to heal;
For the soul to mourn...

All that was lost,
In an instant,
Stealing hopes and dreams.
Upending a foundation,
It took years to build.

Memories ripped from the making...

A life cut short,
Needlessly so...

Tattered,
Shredded,
Drapes...
A once ornate castle;
A far less desired path,
Those left behind...
Must take.

A journey without beloved,
At their side.
Castle,
Soul,
Once lavish,
Languished...
Structural soundness;
Denied.

JLR Spear

Amazing Friend

Time melts away,
As do the cares,
Of the world...
In mind and body,
When I rest here with you.
I am reminded,
Each moment counts.
As too soon I return home,
To robotically exist in all I say and do.

Yet, right now,
I let go of all,
The demands on my time.
This space,
Sacred.
Reserved,
Special,
Only yours and mine.

A stopping point,
To reflect,
Joyfully and cherish,
Your precious life.
Every secret shared,
Priceless,
Unique,
Never again to find.

Inhalation,
Inspiration,
Endlessly touching my soul.
Not just while,
I rest with you...
Of course, you remain with me,
When I go.

I treasure and pursue,
These undistracted,
Moments...
Truly carrying me through...
Pure and potent.

Your friendship,
Far reaching,
From the day we met.
So many years ago...
Through different paths,
Separation,
Tragedies,
We never grew cold.

Nothing can bring you back,
To your actual physical form.
Still,
As I sit here with the shell of you below,
Even in the chill...
Your spirit keeps,
Me held and warm.

We are both,
So independent.
Having chosen,
To do things our own way.
Without much care,
Of judgements,
Or setbacks along the way.

Thank you,
For the moments of peace,
And reprieve,
You give,
I breathe in,
Appreciate you,
My forever,
Existing,
Amazing Friend,

JLR Spear

Appreciation of YOU

I wish I could have been to you,
In life,
What you have been to me...
In death.
I have never given you,
All you have given to me...
Still grieving how you left.

I tried to be there,
For you,
Deep in my own inadequacy...
While you have extended yourself,
Guiding me constantly.

What good could I have possibly done?
To deserve you and your love...
You give tirelessly,
Of your time,
Instead of being enraptured...
Flying above.

I want you to know,
How much I appreciate all that you
were,
And are now...
I accept,
Hold dear,
Any communication with you...

That you so graciously allow.

I hope we continue to share,
Please, never truly leave.
You have held me,
Loved me...
Inspired me,
Kept me,
And made me believe.

JLR Spear

Beneath, Below, High Above

I sit in the sun,
While you lie below.
Yet privileged,
Unleashed,
Is your beautiful soul.

No more do you reach for,
Things beyond your grasp.
You roam at will,
And fly effortlessly at last.

No sadness,
No darkness,
Not an ounce of shame.
We are pitied,
The sad,
The broken framed,
Which here remain.

You whisper,
You move,
You teach us...
If we choose to listen,
With openness and love.

I sit here,
Tethered,
Heavy,
Truly below.
While you ascended,
Rescued,
Existing...
With me...
Even so.

JLR Spear

Birds of the Air

Come,
Sit with me,
Sweet birds of the air.
My heart is grieving,
Broken,
Yet,
I am grateful,
You are all here.

This life has been,
Far more challenging,
Than ever could be explained.
Just the sight...
Of your smooth,
Bright feathers,
Comfort the pain.

Your song,
Soothes the tattered parts.
I watch you paused,
Curiously taking me in,
Quietly enveloping my heart.

Flitting through the air,
As I wish I could...
Delicately,
Yet deliberately with ease.
The deep ache is muted,

For a moment...
When my eyes rest,
Upon you in a nearby tree.

I'll not move.
I'll scarcely breathe...
Oh. Sweet birds of the air,
I pray,
Stay just a while,
With me.

JLR Spear

Change!

Exciting,
Fresh,
Interesting,
Open,
Exhilarating...
Daunting,
Intimidating;
Uncertain,
Frightening.
Perhaps...
Comforting,
Peaceful...
STRANGE!
Hopeful,
Enjoyable,
Excruciating,
Unsettling...
CHANGE!

JLR Spear

Circle of Love

I am in a circle of love,
Ever expanding,
And real.
Surrounded,
Enveloped,
By so many loves gone on;
As well as those here,
I can physically touch,
Hear, and feel.

Dozens of others,
Surround me daily
And I hear,
Those passed on far more clearly.
Sharing life,
Wisdom,
Love and support.
Experiencing laughter,
Warmth and tears.

I am cocooned,
Within a circle of non-physical,
And physical alike.
Never alone,
Always home...
Bathing in wonder...
Unique,
Glorious light.

JLR Spear

Comfort in Grief

Even with much pain,
Discomfort,
Life turned upside down;
Awaiting cosmic generosity,
As I till this weary ground.

Unearthing daily,
Deeper meanings of life,
Discovering inner peace.
Anxiously awaiting...
For sweet release.

The untold,
The unknown,
Blessings bound,
For this soul...trudging earth.
Weeping pours forth,
To moisten the ground,
Due to struggles and trials since birth.

Coming so far,
Gaining spiritual...
Over the natural.
Rising even in grief,
With strength,
Discipline,
Over the habitual.

Knowing unequivocally,
Great goodness and wonder,
On its way to me.
Giving hope,
Inspiration...
Of all that is going to be.

Grabbing at any happiness presented
each day,
I purpose myself,
To receive...
All I was meant to have,
A life lived,
Worthy of me...
Desired for me,
By those lost,
From the day I was conceived.

Greater knowledge gained,
Unlike that which is learned in school;
Gifts of the universe...
Becoming...
Tried and true.

JLR Spear

Cruelty

Pulling,
Ripping,
Tearing at the seams.
Once a vibrant,
Giving,
Loving,
Human being.
Insects gather,
Predators seek,
To devour...
Stealing,
Shaking,
Rattling,
Throughout the hours.

Even with small victories;
Triumph!
Cruelty;
Thy name is Life!
Not enough...
For wait...
Then death comes.

JLR Spear

Dark to Light

It was a tough day for me,
Like the day I wrote you...
Then you died and I didn't know,
For days.
You came to me after the funeral,
In the form of a gentle blowing wind.
A great white egret.
Visiting me on the bank of a lake,
I had gone to for comfort,
Asking for your presence.
You answered me,
Assured me all would be ok,
Eventually...
You then sent me to your gravesite,
To comfort your mother weeping.
We spoke of you and laughed,
Cried hard,
For many hours.
I returned home,
Spent,
Then you whispered again...
"Keep searching",
I did and found you.
Encouraging me further,
I felt your belief in me.
So like you...
Selfless,
Loving,

Hope giving.
I then rested and fell,
Fast asleep.
To awake to my daughter's
Beautiful smile...
And the beauty awaiting outside.
More signs,
More words,
Spoken to me...
Sinking in deep.
You are ever with me,
Pushing me forward,
As you always did.
I am so appreciative,
Of every blessed second...
Making all the difference.
"Rest, breathe,
In the beauty of the moment,
Nothing more important than this.
Be inspired,
Inspiring others", you said...
Just as you did and are.
Sadness falls,
Then falls away...
Realization of the bigger picture.
Like a hawk ascends,
Above the earth,
Seeing what others cannot see.
Embracing dreams often,
As reality.

I have been honored,
Privileged to be visited daily,
By you.
Please,
Always stay close,
And do life with me.
I cannot imagine you ever going away,
Being silent.
I know…
Instinctually,
When you came back into my life,
Before dying,
You would leave…
Drastically.
I could not have known,
How you would return to me,
More powerful than in dreams…
I dreamt before I saw your face again.

Darkness may fall,
Then in time,
The Light shines in.
We are closer in death,
Than we were in life;
Astounding.
I feel chosen,
Special,
Unique...
Thank you,
Most beautiful spirit,
Friend,
Now, always with me.

JLR Spear

Darkness Falls

Darkness falls,
Sun rises.
How many days,
Have passed?
Each one blends,
Into another.
My heart can't,
Keep track.

Since you've left,
This forsaken earth.
So much still,
Remains unseen.
On a blanket,
Over freshly moved dirt.
You lie beneath...
I am here,
Atop.

My heart beats,
Yours, forevermore...
Stopped.

Shouldn't the whole universe,
Halt?!
...at such a loss?
How can everything go on?
Day to day,

As if over the bridge...
You have not crossed?

It's Easter,
How I wish you...
Would resurrect yourself.
Give everyone a joyous gift,
A laugh at death!
Return you back from decay,
To your sleek and svelte self.

Yet, I know you are free,
More than any of us,
Left here.
Without sickness,
Sadness,
Regret or fear.

Still, as the sun,
Rises and sets.
I barely notice at all.
Days seem to turn to weeks,
Months...
As the darkness falls.

JLR Spear

Daughter, Mother Found

Imagining you alive,
Peacefully sleeping...
While you were missing,
Heart,
Furiously beating.

A mother's terror,
When her adult daughter,
Is LOST!
Rest,
Eating...
Cease to exist,
No peace,
No comfort,
Brought.

Only the harsh reality,
Of safety,
Breath...
Of life,
Giving anything.
Searching in the dark of night,
On foot,
Panting,
Just needing her daughter's safety.

The life of that young woman,
Far more precious,

Than a mother's own...
Simply, inconceivable;
She would not make it home.

Warnings came...
Mother remained...
Overwhelmed with pure relief...
Seeing in her mind's eye,
Clear and bright,
This time,
Daughter escaping a wretched fate.

Mother hoping in future,
This young one will take better care,
Of the love and life she bore...
Truth be told,
If the daughter were to do leave before...
The mother;
She would exist in a shell of a life,
Vibrant & strong,
NO more!

JLR Spear

Departed Sweet Friend

I haven't felt you close,
Intensely,
In quite a while,
My dear friend.
Please,
Be near me,
Be with me,
Send love I can feel,
Your support again.

I am distracted,
I know,
By the heaviness,
My soul is under...
Ravaging what peace and strength,
I do find,
No powerful bolt,
Just mere rumble of thunder.

Even more lately,
I need your presence to help pull me up,
To no longer feel submerged,
Beneath other intrusions,
Uninvited...
I beg you strengthen me to re-emerge.

Often you give me what I need,
To turn about.

I do not physically have you with me,
So soulfully,
Give that sweet comfort...
You've brought since you left.
Making this Science minded one...
A "spiritual" convert.

Don't leave me feeling foolish,
You have carried me through,
The most impossible days...

Soul's terror and torrents.
You've lightened,
With fresh breezes,
Kissing my face,
My body feeling suspended,
Less abhorrent.

Return to me,
Once more,
Inspire and breathe into me,
Fill up my lungs.
Inhale and exhale,
Through me once again...
I miss you more than words can say,
My loving,
Imperative,
Though sweetly,
Departed friend.

JLR Spear

Endeavor to Provide YOU Eternal Rest

A warm sunny day,
Walking home from the bus stop,
Underneath the bluest of sky.
Already feeling apprehension,
Though you should have felt safe,
With many others,
Nearby.
Walking home,
Almost there,
Grabbed from the trees,
You strolled near,
Led to some abandoned, burnt home.
Charred,
Gross,
Cruel,
Cold place,

Your killers,
And you,
Alone.
They tried to take what wasn't theirs,
You courageously fought for your virtue.
Yet that was the end of your cries,
Unheard,
As bullets collapsed your struggle...
Harshly ripping through.

You'd been beaten,
Unnecessarily defiled,
Just minutes before almost arriving home.
Your mom waited anxiously,
Unlike you to be gone...
She called the police as the minutes ticked
by,
Something,
Definitely wrong!

Parents, loved ones,
Community rocked to the core,
Violence so unjust!
Even still,
25 years later,
They have never been caught,
Killers could still...
Be among us.
I cannot let you go,
The thought of you so young,
And life...ended.
You fought,
Resisted,
Full of integrity,
Exactly what you were valiantly living.
Sweet,
Beautiful,
Innocent soul...
So many years have passed now,

*I just can't understand why I can't let you
go.*

*Now, I have a daughter,
The age you were...
When you were maliciously taken,
Violently removed from the earth...
She is just as kind and pure?
It does not matter...
Why I can't let go,
You are a sister of mine.
I just can't believe there has been no
justice...
To those responsible this heinous crime.
I am here,
Even now...
To listen if you'd like to share.
Any helpful information,
To catch the murderers...
I am attentive,
Alert.
I will receive,
Any details you want me to know,
I will research and follow,
With diligence and fervor.*

*Your family,
Our town,
Deserve to know...
Who walks among us?*

With darkness at heart,
Those secrets to be shown.
You will receive,
If I have anything to do with it,
Retribution after all.
Killers will be caught,
Exposed,
Brought to justice,
I pray...
And most assuredly they will fall!
Disgraced,
Dishonored,
Brought from where they hide.
You were,
Are... so precious a girl?
I will continue to try!

I want to reveal them
Help heal this community...
I am here and listening.
I will return to your bus stop.
Retrace your steps,
Visit all the places,
Especially where you were put to sleep...
Tears falling,
Heart wide open,
Lead me to assist in the hunt,
Their capturing...
Providing your parents and sibling with
closure...
Endeavoring to provide rest to you,
eternally!

JLR Spear

Eternal Embrace of My Son

Stepping into the light,
For the first time,
Absorbing rays of sunlight.
Warmth,
Change from the chill,
Of grief.
Anguish subsides,
Enters;
Belief.

I will survive.
I will go on.
I will regain,
An awkward form of normal,
Growing strong.

Though ever-altered,
Now holding a different view;
Point of reference,
Slightly askew.

Wailing has ceased,
For a time...
To enter into a reformed,
Design...

Way of living and being,
Forever changed.

Transformed me feels...
Bizarre and strange.

I will become accustomed to,
A life touched deeply...
Yet now without,
You.

Being physically present,
However,
You always are a past, present, and
future part of me...
Distant,
Yet close,
Radiant,
Constant,
Though, indistinct.

Forming forward abundant life,
With memories...
I am continuously warmed,
By your gracious light;

Constructing,
Combining,
Coalescing,
All into one,
I am ready now...
Stepping into,
Life supernaturally lit...
In the eternal embrace of my son.

JLR Spear

Everlasting Vibrant Life

I still remember,
Your kind touch and smile...
As we sang praise songs at Trinity.
Little did I know
Those precious moments,
Among others,
Would have to last me for eternity.

A beautiful life,
So full,
Cut short by the most,
Darkest means.
Your songs would have to echo,
In hearts you reached,
Without your physical vocal abilities.

Those who took from you,
Dead inside,
Yet lived on.
You gave in sweet love,
And freedom,
Though physically gone.

You're hurting,
Haunted,
Loving,
Wonderful parents still hold close,
To the days you were here.

Your sister,
Steadfast and strong,
To find those who snuffed out your life,
With sadness and tears.

I won't stop believing,
With the community,
Justice will be served.
An entire,
Once sleepy town,
Confused...
Even years later,
Not much has been learned.

I feel you'll tell,
From the grave,
What is not known?
The men,
On earth still,
Will suffer and pay,
Yet not just in this life,
Alone.

A gentle child,
A gracious soul,
Departed from this land.
Harsh and hard the horrendous act,
Yet, Assured...
Her entrance into Heaven;
Grand.

From the future never lived,
Gone and never to be retrieved
Many of us here left wondering,
What was it all for?
Still seeking and trying,
To one day settle the unrighteous,
Uneven score.

Those left behind will assure...
Pure honor and praise...
Will be proclaimed for her!

Keeping her memory alive,
Rooting out her perpetrators,
Almost thirty years later.

That glorious girl would have been 41 this
year,
And perhaps could have had a daughter,
Or a son...
A husband loving and true.
Singing, attending church with family
and friends,
Abounding with hopes of personal success,
No doubt would have ensued.

So many friends from high school,
Would have shared in her
accomplishments,

She would have been Prom Queen.
A Student Government President,
Perhaps...

Captain of the cheerleaders,
Graduated top of her class,
Such honor brought to her family,
What we have all imagined.

We honor her in our hearts,
Non-stop,
Seeking those who snuffed out,
Violently,
A brilliant life.
Yet those men could never take away...
All she was and continues to be...
An inspiration,
Everlasting Vibrant light.

JLR Spear

Extraordinary You

Your adorable button nose,
Freckles,
Perfectly placed.
Bright brown eyes,
Mischievous grin,
Upon your beautiful face.
Long,
Dark flowing hair...
Shiny and wildly,
Flung.
So animated,
So full of life,
Much laughter you'd bring.
Affectionate,
Palpable strength...
Compassion abundant.

You were present,
For those in need.
Any time,
Anywhere.
Your friends,
Never doubted your love...
Your raspy, deep voice a comfort.
Sharing heartaches,
And fun with you,
One always felt heard.
Yet,

I wonder who was truly there,
For one so giving?
To repay all you were,
Wonder if they appreciate you now?
As you are no longer among the living.
I think it so sad,
Hard to believe it true...
You were amazing,

Rare,
Precious,
Extraordinary YOU!!

You have been so close in heart,
All of these years.
I searched and searched for you,
You must have felt me calling out to you,
For suddenly you appeared.

I was granted another year,
So endearing in my life.
Your thoughts,
Your triumphs,
Your failures,
Your love,
You were able to share before,
You said goodbye.
I was finally able to convey,
The power you gave this heart.
Just knowing you and the time we spent,

In each other's presence,
Yet now once again,
We are apart.
I still feel you,
Hear you,
Cannot separate...
That which has been pulled together,
By faith and by fate.
I am so happy we had,
Those moments...
Not long ago.
We left nothing unsaid,
No holds barred...
How could we know?
Our spirits did somehow,
Discern we may not get another try...
For now I sit at your grave,
And just collapse over you as I cry.

No one was like you!
From the moment we met...
From the first time we shared a smile,
A laugh;
Our friendship was solidly set.
My sister,
In this life and in the next.
How extremely fortunate for me,
I was astonished by all I would get.
The uniqueness of you,
Forever, 30 years ago today...

And evermore.
What a short time,
Never enough.
Until I see you again,
I must endure.
I must be satisfied,
Feeling you in the breeze,
Seeing you fly...

In the winds of a butterfly,
Flitting from flowers to trees.
Sensing you when I am alone,
Or with others as the sun touches my skin.
Noticing,
Acknowledging...
Enjoying your presence,
Without an end.
You live with me and me with you.
Death only somehow strengthens,
This bond.
You are not erased,
Forgotten,
Or gone!
You are alive,
More so than me...
Only now you have begun your song.
You are here,
You are with me,
YOU live on!
Many roses and carnations,

Snap dragons,
Tossed upon your coffin,
As your casket descended.
Heart wrenching goodbye,
Tears of all your loved ones...
Voices,
Cries,
Ascended...
To where you are now,
Above,
As well as all around,
Below, and beneath.
A life of love,
Devotion,
Laughter,
Loyalty...
You did bequeath...

To all who were privileged enough,
To know the real you inside.
Those who listened,
And came to you,
Believing you'll never truly die.
You live on in our hearts,
In our breathing,
Memories.
With the same magnitude,
If not more,
We all receive...
All that you were,

And all that you are becoming!
We await the day,
We see you again...
The grandest of all Homecomings!

JLR Spear

Feel at Home

The body is broken,
In pain and so tired.
The weight of so much,
Happening in the world.
Smothers a little,
Of the inward fire.

Recently,
Lost oved ones,
Brings sadness...
With many tears.
Yet, this trial stricken,
Spirit will not fear!

Breathing continues,
Blessings still abound.
Within and in the eyes of others,
Present and while,
There are none around...

This soul,
Is thankful,
In the peace of this moment, alone.
For here,
Anywhere with love of others,
God and self,
I feel at home.

JLR Spear

Forever Closed Door

Deafening blow...
Past rises to suppress.
Failures,
Of not asserting myself...
I must confess.

From a wee child,
Taught to stay quiet,
Even with the inappropriate,
Behaviors toward me...
Including violence.
Though thankfully much healed,
Through may years of therapy,
And self-empowerment and discovery.

Yet still oppressed at times by haunts.
Seeking wisdom,
Though triggered;
Memories crash in to taunt...

Me once again,
Lack of support,
Protection...
Surreal.
Not only me,
And the perpetrator involved,
Others who knew and did nothing...
Darkening the feel.

God, angels,
Loved ones crossed over,
Guide me with love and acceptance...
To stand up...
Be counted,
With worthiness and perseverance.
Deserving of being fought for,
As a child,
Young lady,
As a woman defending with resistance,
No one had the right,
To abuse me,
Or jade my innocence.

I am a precious,
Beautiful,
Wonder to be loved,
Appreciated,
Accepted...
To be cherished,
Held,
Kept,
Protected.
Help me to do so,
For myself,

First and foremost.
Help me heal,
Rise above,
Forgive and let go.
To shut that door and chain it up,
Forever to be closed.

JLR Spear

Frightened Feathered Friend

Sweet,
Wonderful,
Little feathered friend,
Nestled in the folds...
Of drapes hung outside.
Seeking refuge,
From the raging storm,
Blowing in,
You've found a safe sanctuary,
In which you may hide.

Waiting patiently,
For hours through the night,
Lit with lightning,
And rolls of vibrating thunder.
You are safe,
Secure,

Hidden,
Beneath the canopy...
You are under.

I understand wee one.
I seek shelter when things feel,
Uncertain and new...
Then rise and leave the sanctuary,

I have found...
As you will, too.

I will arise to find you have left,
Your comforting space...
So I will go forth as well,
From my hiding place.

Renewed,
Refreshed,
Rested,

Having been secured,
Away from the storm.
Able to face the day,
Instantaneously,
Calm and warmed.

All will be okay,
Even when it seems it isn't...
Light will return.
Once daylight shines,
We will fly once again,
And in magnificence,
Emerge.

JLR Spear

Girl Gone Missing

There was a shooting nearby,
Where you crashed the car,
Fled on foot.
No doubt confused,
Concussed,
Panicked,
Not even knowing,
Where you exactly stood.

A day later,
As you escaped death,
You still did not realize...
How blessed you truly are,
To have survived,
Mostly unharmed,
Alive.

There was so much,
That could have,
Incredibly,
Gone wrong.
Yet you remain,
Breathing,
Largely untouched,
And strong.

I can only hope,
In the days and months to come;

You'd see,
Car demolished,
So much to pay and tend to,
Yet you emerged,
Thankfully...

Your life was spared,
Returning to us safe and sound.
Through woods you wandered,
Aimlessly for hours,
On treacherous ground.

You made it back,
Found your way,
Though completely unaware.
Through danger,
Darkness,
Wired fencing in bushes,
Crime ridden places...
Of despair.

You appeared,
Came back,
Do you understand?
I hope this registers deep.

You were kept safe,
Protected,
Returned,
To a peaceful, living sleep.

Seconds,
Situations,
Away from leaving us....
Please, learn wisdom from all.
Transcend,
Choose well,
Be mindful,
Believe,
Trust.

My wishes,
To a most beautiful daughter,
In faith...

Make changes,
Be aware,
Encouraged,
Be inspired,
Be Truly,
Awake!

JLR Spear

Good Bye

I am learning,
Goodbye is just that...
Good and bye...
In physical form,
For now.
Walking life no different,
No absence,
More presence felt.
Peace of you,
To the wellbeing and leading,
And guiding me,
As well.
Consideration of the night,
To the fresh morning dew,
Not a moment for the rest of our lives,
Physical and non-physical,
Will I be apart from you?

Guarding,
Loving,
Advising,
Each and every day,
No matter circumstances...
Of why you went from earth,
Along your way.

You take me with you and share...
And I take you with me.
Good bye is just that...
Good...
For you...
And the "bye",
Is never truly to be.

JLR Spear

Good Girl!

As a child,
Much grief,
When her father went away.
No, he didn't leave,
He died...
Changing this little girl,
In almost every way.

No more hugs,
Or pats on the head,
With a "good girl",
Her mother became angry,
Depressed he left,
Nothing remained the same,
In their worlds.

The girl moved,
Uprooted from all,
Of her family and loved ones.
Another major life change,
As well as maturity,
Has begun.

Her mother so fearful,
Clenched onto her daughter,
Far too tightly.
A loving, funny soul,
With so much pain,

Trying hard to reject the fighting.

All she wanted was love,
A soft place,
Some fun...
And to hear,
"Good girl",
Once again.
Her family.
So intricately
Entwined in her life,
Still her heart was most comfortable,
With her best friend.

Sneaking out,
Seeking adventure,
Underneath the mother's nose.
She found places to freely be herself.
Dancing,
Roaming the beaches,
Acting,
Writing prose.
Trying so hard to balance
New-found secretive freedom,
With the controlling home.

She still missed her father,
Always,

Needing more love and comfort,

From her mother,
Yet, felt vastly alone.

Was she a reminder of him?
The mother had remarried.
Still,
How could that be a bad thing?
Painful as it may be.

Only one or two knew the pain...
She felt,
Beneath the hilarious jokes.
Friends, like me...
Deep into the teens,
Were there listening,
Encouraging her to let go.

No matter how hard this
Sweet girl tried,
She could not...
We didn't know how deep,
She shared so much,
Feeling privileged,
The chosen few would keep,

Secrets to the grave,
In my presence,
In my wedding,
She was continually adored.
So innocent, wise,

Sultry,
Perfectly her.
She far more than her mother,
Would ever give her credit for.

We lost touch for a few years.
As we went along different paths.
I, married with children,
She, absolutely free,
Chose a college of Psychology, the Arts,
And Math.

I sought her out...
Prayed she would return,
And she did now and then.
She was always in my thoughts,
Little did I know?
The inner pain of childhood,
Had never stopped.

Unaware, I was...
That my dear friend was in so much,
Inner turmoil.

When together,
It was all fun and games,
I didn't know alone,
She'd re-coil.

Perhaps,

I took it all too lightly;
The times she shared our scars...
Perhaps,
I was too distracted by diapers, bottles,
And my only little ones being afraid of
the dark.

I just hate I didn't know,
She began to turn and hide.
She would vanish yet again,
Finding chemicals rather than friends,
More available to make her feel "high".

We once experienced that feeling,
Together,
Young, with our lives lying fully ahead,
Without chemicals needed in the vein.
Friendship created that...
And it was enough for us.
At that time,
It was all pure,
Though her mother spoke the worst of her,
Innocent she was.

Over time,
More adulthood and disappointments,
As well as the harassment of her mom,
The names she called this sweet girl,
She unfortunately became...
Almost as if she had no choice,

Falsely accused constantly,
Running, broken, in pain.

My heart is broken,
That she was continuously treated so.
She began a life of crime.
Jailed, reduced,
Crying out,
Yet, why didn't I,
Her closest friend,
"Feel it" all this time.

She never left my dreams,
I continued to search for her.
Finally, she found me months after a
dream.
She knocked on many doors,
Down my street,
Looking for me.

She came in and she shared,
Bared all,
And we became close once more.

In and out of the hospital,
Sending her flowers and prayer,
And lots of love... to endure!

Many hours of conversation out back,
Laughing,

Pictures,
Playful and mischievous talk.
Men chasing her all over the place,
Her travel,
My divorce, and my adult children
moved on.

She and my youngest bonded,
Glad to share each other's joy.
Many hours,
So much laughter and tears,
We enjoyed.

She had just contacted me,
Three days before,
It wasn't uncommon for her to be a ghost,
For a day or two.
Then my heart sank deep,
Into the earth,
When her mother pulled into my drive
way,
Told me what I moments before,
Felt and knew.

Something told my heart,
She had left the earth,
The second the mother,
Entered my drive.
Shocked,
I wailed,

Held onto to her...
Screamed, and cried.

My life forever changed that day,
As well as her mother's.
She had died the overdose death,
Tragically,
As the pain was too great for her to
cover.

Deep, heart wrenching pain,
I had found the little stuffed bear,
Her dad gave her,
And she gave it to me, long ago.
Instead of being able to give it back to
her.
In person,
I had to set it in her coffin with her...
And watch as she was taken from me,
Down below.

Tossing roses,
Hitting the wood of the box,
Devastating to hear.
There was no haunting to,
The moaning of all and endless,
Painful tears.

Weeks later,
Alone,

After much mourning at her gravesite.
I closed my eyes,
Prayed to her...
And feel I received great insight.

She was too precious,
Too innocent in heart,
With too much pain...
For this world...

She once again,
Finally got to go to her father,
Hearing...
"YOU ARE MY GOOD GIRL"!

Too bad she never heard,
What she needed from...
Those now left behind,
We cannot control what other's do,
Yet we can choose to do our part in being
kind.

I told her she was amazing,
Intelligent,
Beautiful,
Smart,
Though it may have not been enough,
In the end,
There was no question of her place,
In my heart.

And I say;
I LOVE YOU FOREVER "GOOD GIRL",
Doesn't matter you lost your way.
I will see you once again,
Embrace you then,
And once again,
We will laugh like young girls at play.

JLR Spear

Grief Likened to a Hurricane

Perhaps you felt,
The pressure drop.
Your emotions and body,
Somehow aware of a coming storm.
Tuned in...
Soul and spirit,
May have given you a forecast.
Still you were taken aback,
Gasped and sideswiped,
When your loved ones passed.

Inside you,
Squalls became apparent,
Wind, rain,
Lightning...
Maybe even a tornado...
That sent you running,
Deep inside yourself,
And your faith...
As you could hear,
The gusts violently blow.

In between the squalls,
Some rest...
Reprieve,
A bit of sunshine.

Then once again,
Quit rapidly...
All at once,
You find...

You're in that place again,
For a time.
A feeling inside,
You are home.
Earth then rattles,
Beneath you once again...

More nerve racking noise,
Trembling.

The eye then takes its time passing over,
And you step outside.
Breathe deep,
Then peace gives way as the powerful,
Slamming wall of the hurricane hits.
Yet now you know,
The worst will be over soon,
And you will live.

So you take it on,
As it gives way...
Knowing over time the winds,
Will cease to cause the trees to sway;
You'll ride the squalls once more,
And take the breaks in between...

When you'll enjoy the blue skies,
And sun again...
With the still undisturbed, vibrant trees
of green.
Birds chirping,
You can hear them,
As the storms leave...
You exit the safe house into calm,
Peaceful surroundings.

The process is all achieved,
With time...
Reflection...
And letting go...
Eventually,
The deep sadness and grief.

In time you realize,
You are stronger,
Growing closer to the loved one...
Resting,
At peace.
Assured one day you will join,
Others as well,
When all is said and done.

You find,
They've never left your side...
Just physically gone.
Spiritually with you,

Stronger than ever...
Helping you feel more secure,
As you move on.

Then you share the laughs,
Memories,
Good times...
And thoughts of the past,
As well as the sunshine...
Created inside your soul with friends,
Here and now!

You survived the hurricane,
You stand secure....
With your loved one nearer,
On firmer,
Solid ground.

JLR Spear

Heart in a Noose

Wriggle,
Squirm,
Struggle all you will...
Only tightens and pulls,
Tighter,
Even still.

Reach your fingers,
Underneath...
Tighter,
No relief!

You've spent your efforts,
Moments,
To untie...
Everything you've experienced,
Multiplies...

The intensity,
Feeling,
You'll never be released.
Mind,
Heart,
Body,
All deceived.

Efforts,
All for naught.

Each second,
Seemingly securing,
The knot.

A mental trapeze...
Attempts to help another,
Trying to assist a child suffering,
Not some random other.

Giving up now,
Not a choice.
As it gets tighter...
Losing your voice.

Tethered forever,
You've settled,
You must endure abuse.
If only you could somehow loose,
Your life,
Your heart,
Effectively,
From the noose.

JLR Spear

Hindered, No more!

It wasn't you,
Lying in that casket...
Cold, rigid,
Blank.
Warmth of you,
Laughter, smiles,
Beauty...
Even less than faint.

Strange, I didn't feel grief,
For the moment,
Rather, I rejoiced.
Realizing you truly are free,
No longer there...
My heart began to pound loudly,
As I heard your voice:

"I no longer weep,
I am with you always...
Joyous and flying high.
This is a chapter that is bitter for you,
Sweet for me,
So do not cry.

I am in the breeze,
That touches your hair,
In the warmth of sweet memories.
Unchained.

Unencumbered,
A butterfly,
The sun on your face,
A green, living,
Shade giving tree.

Body beneath,
No longer needed.
I'm not held back in any way.
Free to roam the realms,
Wishing you were here with me,
As children we would play.

I'll see you again,
Dear friend...
And hold you close as before.
When you at last are free,
Just as I am,
You will be...
Hindered no more!"

JLR Spear

Hope is Hope

The night settles in,
Bones sore.
I retreat,
Awaiting...
The vibrancy of a new day,
To admire and meet.

Possibilities within...
The human mind,
Dreams of new love,
Laughter,
And a kinder sunshine.

I am not sure if it,
Will truly come,
Still I feel hope for that which today...
Has undone.

Hope To be rebirthed,
And become well once again,
A hope is hope...
And it is all I have,
As this day...
Most assuredly must end.

JLR Spear

In Need of Abundance

Abundance of good,
I bid you to come...
Crashing as an energetic wave,
Upon our shore;
Giving life,
Exuberance,
Plenty...
As never before.

Shake the ground,
As new life reaches,
From the earth.
A vibrant display of charity,
New birth.

You have long been awaited,
By myself and my seed...
Returning forth the multiplied,
Precious,
Pure,
And innocent deeds.

Returning much given,
Past and present...
All that is wonderful,
Expected,
And pleasant!
Much more will be given of course,
Over and over again...
Springing forth,
Bubbling up and out,
Overflowing;
Abundance.

JLR Spear

Instinct

Instinct alerted me,
Our time together,
Was short.
I felt,
You would soon leave.
As much,
As I preferred,
To deny...
The tugging in my heart,
Prompted me...

I let go,
Of all bounds,
And told you all I felt.
Your place in my life,
In my heart.
All between us,
Became beautiful and well.

Now,
Instinct,
Dear one,
Alerts me once more,
For another sweet friend,
Who has struggled?
I've spoken,
The same to him,
But gave him the warning,

I'd not given to you,
And he was troubled.

Yet, he said he'd take care,
Realizing my love and concern.
He'd stay aware,
Refrain from same errors and endeavor,
To believe more,
To love and learn.

Today,
When I saw his mother's number,
A called missed.
I was filled with dread,
I haven't forgotten,
Your mom in my drive way,
Crying out,
"My daughter is dead".

I choose here forward not to fear,
I'm cautioned,
Not wanting another life consumed.
Every moment with loved ones,
Precious,
I appreciate all with gratitude.

I pray to God,
Keep him safe,
Let my words have strengthened,
His resolve...

As he lives and changes,
Take him not.
May he rather in breathing,
Here in this life,
Evolve.

Thankfully my friend's mother,
Was just calling to check on me.
When loss is prevalent,
Too often...
Sometimes it is hard,
To know when it is apprehension,
Or Instinct.

JLR Spear

Introspective Challenges

We all struggle,
To get through life,
With healthy coping skills,
And some vices.
Doing what we feel,
Is the best...?
Coping with many different
circumstances,
In crisis.

We can only hope to reach,
For peace to be there in some,
Tangible form.
Most challenging ties can cause us to
escape,
However different from our norm.

Stilling the soul in chains,
Not an easy feat.
Yet it is worth our quiet retreat,
Into the introspection of ourselves,
To find strength and passion,
To erect from the deep.

We all tire of the challenges,
Difficult roads which may lay ahead;
Increasingly so as we get older,
Imagining it would be easier,

Somehow...
Yet instead...
Although many factors complicate,
And flood the ground,
Progress and forward motion,
We find comes from delving further
down.

Some achieve it faster than others,
Some fail,
Some resilient,
Finding a way out...

Overcoming inexperience,
Deficits,
Grief and self-doubt.

We try moment by moment,
Finding failure does not make us less.
Hopefully,
We arise to try once again...
To one day obtain the security,
Stability,
Which we all deserve;
A final place on this earth,
Of peace and rest.

JLR Spear

Looming, Daunting...Not Today

Set forth,
Toward another day...
To conquer,
Nay,
Tackle,
So much to do.
Then weariness of all,
So daunting,
Comes to suppress you.

Then settling in,
Decide "Okay, not today,
After all".
As so much looming ahead,
Seems to grow increasingly tall.

The process cannot be rushed;
Hurried along.
It takes time to dismantle,
Re-build,
Into a new type of strong.

Inward to outward,
This time specifically for oneself,
Eventually spilling all the wonder gained,
Coming through the grief,

Pouring onto everyone else.

Another day,
Perhaps...
A nibble...
Just a bit will get done.
Although now it is evident,
Today will not be the ONE.

JLR Spear

Loose the Noose

Today...
You rest,
Maybe create,
Maybe hold onto hope...
That tomorrow won't come forth,
To strangle you,
With its tightening rope.

Around the neck,
Hands, and feet,
Figuratively speaking...
With worries of this life.
Today though,
You won't worry,
Set off to enjoy some kind of
Blue sky;
That may inspire,
Enliven somehow...
Cutting the rope binding you.
Anything is possible,
After all with belief,
Finding a solution way...
And thus loosening the noose.

JLR Spear

Low

Most days,
Lively enough,
To rise up to challenges,
Pain, and such.
Life is just that way,
So press in,
Press on,
Does it really amount to much?

Some days,
It is just too difficult to keep,
Head above...
The waters that rise in others;
Greed,
Hate,
Imbalance of...
Their excessive self-love.

Trying to stay atop it all,
With a positive outlook,
To keep moving full steam ahead.
Still, the heaviness,
Can darken the skies,
Takeover
Seep in.

Some days,
Resources seem unavailable...

To combat,
A moment longer.
Lately every effort is exhausted,
Surrendered...
Awaiting a rising sun of a new day...
To make stronger.

Knowing many must struggle,
As well...
Knowing,
Not alone.
Yet, as the days go by,
Forgetting sometimes...
All strength manages to grow.

In disdain,
Somber moments,
Hardest to overcome.
Affording anyway...
There goes another day,
Tainted and undone.

Learning eventually,
Movement forward,
In time with an increased,
Sustained pace...

For now accepting today's
Defeat,
Brought low,
Crawling back to a hide-away.

JLR Spear

Message Received

Still,
Completely,
In shock.
So much taken,
Ravaged,
Tilted and rocked...
Spewed uncontrollably,
Onto me.
Wonder what I have done,
To deserve...
This state of being.

Reached out,
And having given,
More than I had.
Learned all about boundaries,
To stave away the bad.

Having been all,
I could possibly be,
To others and myself.
Yet, unable to deny the continued
suffering,
Of the hand I've been dealt.

I have called forth the promises,
Shown honesty in love...
Denied myself,

Honored others first,
When push came to shove.

I watched in sadness,
As others through evil gained ground,
While I lost it.
Still managed to find peace,
Giving,
Gratitude of good presented,
Found.

Balance,
Harmony,
Truth...
I continually seek.
Though greeted with hate,
Disdain,
Defeat.

Confused,
I continue to be me,
Live,
Love,
All that I possibly can.
I wait and wonder when
I'll be delivered,
From the horrid works of men.

I pray for those who speak ill of me.
Without malice,

Hate,
Without any desire to compete.

Closing to light the slights,
Insults,
Abuse,
Up like a flame...
Within a prayer,
Not having allowed such things,
As verbalized disgust,
To dismantle the sane.

God,
When will I be?
Just treated well...
Provided for...
I refuse to be a victim,
Or martyr...
Just needing more.

Sometimes it feels,
My prayers fall upon deaf ears.
"My love,
No longer allow it",
I am here to give you courage,
And I do care,
I do hear."

JLR Spear

Natural Feel of Home

The body is broken,
In pain...
So tired.
The weight of so much,
Happening in the world.
Smothers some,
The inward fire.

Recently,
Lost oved ones,
Brings sadness...
With many tears.
Yet, this trial stricken,
Spirit will not fear!

Breathing continues,
Blessings still abound.

Within and in the eyes of others,
Present,
Even when no others...
Are around.

This soul,
Is thankful,
In the peace of the moment, alone.
For here and anywhere...
Just God and myself,

I feel at home.

Love, laughter,
A safe place to fall.
Protection...
Boundaries,
And Space...
Created to get away from it all...

To feel the grass,
Beneath my feet,
To hear sweet birds,
Chirp nearby.
To wonder and gaze,
Upon bees and dragon flies.

Reuniting the soul,
With the creation that gave birth,
To intrinsic love.
I grasp for serenity,
A Quiet time,
With precious trust...

That the setting sun,
Will bring forth,
The possibility of a splendid day.

Where I may live,
Laugh,
And peacefully fall,
With nature in comfort,
Another day!

JLR Spear

No Control

You can try to help,
Again and again,
Yet free will of another,
Pushes back.
Regardless of time,
Energy,
Love,
Forgiveness,
And money spent...
One chooses lack.

Finding,
Their inner anger,
Refusing...
With verbal abuse,
Something intangible,
Spiritual or mental,
Keeping one from the truth.

I've done all I can do,
I bless and pray for them.
Yet they wish me away,
Ill will...
Remaining nasty and grim.

I hope one day,
In love,
They will allow,

Inner-self to speak and reveal...
Revelation to soul,
Acceptance of truth,
Honesty,
Transformation which heals.

For now (Sigh)...
Exhale,
And let go of all control...

Having none,
Still, I must allow myself,
To be consoled.

Somehow find rest and peace,
What I set about to complete;
Others will be who and what they are,
No matter how it affects me.

Finding a way,
I pray,
Souls, though broken,
Move on...
Diminished,
Yet learning,
Will emerge and become strong.

Only the individual,
Can allow the choices of others,
To grieve the mind...

Release,
Let go...
Heal...
I chose to remain,
Thoughtfully truthful and kind.

I will speak wisdom still,
Though it may be disregarded.
Lessons to be learned by others...
Cannot be borne by me,
Leaving me ill guarded.

Healthy boundaries,
Will protect you and aid,
Though others may choose calamity.

Being the keeper of only me,
Among fallen hopes and dreams,
And often insanity.

Pressing on in the midst,
Of all that has been taken.
My loved one and me,
I hold close to...
Regardless of fear,
Sadness,
And shaking.

Learning the lessons I alone,

Am able to learn,
Praying best for all,
Continually,
Protection,
Blessings,
Love,
Will one day be returned?

Fulfilled in the best way,
Yet only as others will allow.
When having done my best,
Rest,
Breathe,
Exhale.
No control...
Finding peace on my own,
Whether those around me,
Triumph or fail.

JLR Spear

Ode to an Innocent Soul

Your bright smile,
Kind and caring eyes.
Helped people feel free...
To be themselves,
And you... so inviting.
Spirit untethered,
Happy,
Sweet yet interesting,
Exciting.
You're spirit,
Flits above us all,
In infinite wonder.
No one could ever,
Take what you have given,
In life or even six feet under.
With every breath,
While you were here,
You gave,
Became a priceless part of God's plan.
No one,
Not even those horrid men,
Could erase your precious innocence,
An eternal, protected gift,
Far above mere mortal man.
You still comfort so many,
With even the mere thought of who you
were...

Now even more powerful,
Your faith and essence,
Endure.
Your life and image,
Never tainted,
No matter how you passed.
No one could replace your pure goodness,
Life eternal,
Will forever last.

JLR Spear

One Gruesome, Strange Catastrophe

Time after time,
Day after day,
Year after year...
Misfortune,
Heartache,
Distaste,
Seems to visit here.

Much good done,
So why the curse?
Healing offered to others,
Given gifts,
Gratitude for all...
Yet, immersed;

Plunged,
Rather,
Into darkness created by others.
I've been present,
Helpful,
Now turn to friends,
To help me recover.
Lives lost,
Cruelty,
Undeserved struggle,
Challenges,

When will I be free?

From all the years I have given;
And yet receive...
Life as one,
Gruesome...
Strange,
Catastrophe!

JLR Spear

Only Best Thoughts of You

Some have said of you,
"Too many demons",
Were in your mind.
I feel,
You are light,
Beautiful,
Kind...
Unique,
And now in death,
Have left supposed "demons" behind.

I only feel goodness,
Towards you now,
Thankful of our time together,
For the love you have brought...

To this earth,
To my life,
And to so many.
Only the BEST thoughts,
Of you...
Unending.

JLR Spear

Only to Crawl

I am beginning to ignore,
The chest tightening,
The strangled feeling,
The deafening screams,
All beginning to silence me.
Hate spewed forth,
Like a destructive dragon's fiery breath,
Singeing everything within,
Each day.
I hope,
I pray,
And do my best.
Yet it's getting harder,
Once again...
To feel peaceful rest.
Every muscle tenses and cries out.
Again...

I'll ignore.
Even though deep,
Deep down,
I can take no more.

These words I have uttered,
Written ...so many times,
Years before.
The strides I make,
To lessen each and every resistance,

Somehow...
Profoundly becomes more.

Not afraid of changes,
Offer many...
On a daily basis...
Giving sweetness,
Kindness,
And patience.

Then I feel the breath,
Huffing hot upon my neck,
Invoking something I won't give...
Allowance for treatment of this kind,
Ever again.
Simply,
I am learning to walk away,
Allowing all else but me to be singed.
Protecting myself,
Timing out of the dysfunction,
Removing myself,
From that which becomes unhinged.

Time away shows me,
My words,
Self,
Mean something,
Then upon return...

In an instant,

I am yanked and twisted,
Contorted to something else,
Never intended.

Light,
Love,
Generosity of spirit,
I bring to this home...
Immediately upended.
What could I possibly be missing?
When having given my all?
Another sun rises,
I set about to let it go...
Believe,
Share,
And Give...
Only to crawl.

JLR Spear

Pondering Why You Left

I know you suffered,
Pain in your body and mind.
I sensed you would leave this world,
And me... far behind.
Yet,
Was it intentional?
Or an accidental overdose?
I seek,
Search,
And hope to find answers,
Though there isn't a physical one...
Perhaps a spiritual last love note?
One which you did not leave,
Making many think,
It just went all wrong.
Did you intend to leave this earth?

Or chase away your pain,
For a moment... to feel strong?
I'll endeavor,
To find the truth,
Even though my heart says "no",
I just need to have this closure,
Eventually, to discover...
Which way you meant to go.

JLR Spear

Ponderings of a Weary Heart

There is a comfort,
A calm,
With the crickets' song,
As the day settles down,
And darkness falls.

The cool of the breeze,
Not present in the former day.
Perhaps now the cleansing storm,
Will wash all dust away...

From the heart and mind,
Which toils onward on this earth;
As creatures emerge upon the dampened,
Chilled dirt.

The sun will rise,
And a new day will start...
For the soul,
The earth,
And the weary heart.

JLR Spear

Psychosomatic Cyclical War

Emotional upset,
Confusion,
Difficult to explain...
Continual solutions,
Applied,
Fade to gray.

Healthy habits to implement,
Day to day feats,
To win and move...
Yet more commonly known...
Defeat!

Education,
Information,
Best of all intentions...

Only to succeed for a moment,
Too soon becoming failed interventions.

There is a cost...
Stomach shrivels in protest,
Head feeling racked and slain.
Stressors produce,
The least desired response...
Adversely affecting the brain.

Mind and body,
Fight for reasons...
Pushed and pulled,
To the core...
Environmental,
Internal reality...
Begets this individual's,
Psycho-somatic,
Cyclical War!!!

JLR Spear

Reflective Peace

Reflective Peace
Waters,
Calming breeze.
Rolls in;
Ripples.
Satisfied,
In the Pure,
The simple.

Muddy mind,
Washed clean,
At ease.
Sun dances,
Upon small waves,
Reflective Peace.

JLR Spear

Reopened Old Wounds

Time passes,
We press on,
We change.
We move forward...
Expecting best in ourselves,
And others.

A planned or chance meeting occurs...
Face to face with our past,
Suddenly,
Feeling uncovered,
Our jolt of pain,
We mask.

We gathered for a purpose,
Hoping for a peaceful exchange,
Of pleasantries...

Believing,
All has changed.

Finding rather,
Some individuals devolve,
Inflicting further harm.
Met on occasion,
With immediate, recurrent damage.
Unexpectedly opening sores,
Sounding an alarm.

Acknowledging with disappointment,
A freshly wounded heart...
Resilience learned,
Conquering still...
Though extremely hard...

Forgiving,
Walking away,
Heart in our hands...
To pause...
Regain composure and stand.

Realizing,
No one can take our resolve,
None can destroy the reformed versions
of us.
Boundaries erected,
While continuing to process...

Introspection to Improve,
Disallowance of further injury.
To a now more opened,
Wound...
Still healing.

JLR Spear

Reprieve

The laughter of a child,
A comforting smile of a dear friend.
A glass of deep,
Oakey red wine,
On the porch at day's end.
Chill of the morning,
Birds awakening with a new day.
There is beauty in this life,
Come what may...
Through hardships,
And trials,
I choose to focus on comforts;
That which brings joy and will appease...
The ache of great sorrows,
Soothing the soul,
Providing much needed...
Reprieve.

JLR Spear

Resilience of an Eternal Soul

Deep loss of a child,
An only precious child.
Loss of mother and father as well,
All experienced too close together.
Through a pandemic,
Through burrows deep,
And penetrating...
The soul arises.
Harnessing the strength,
For child still spiritually present...

Lending energy and joy...
Not otherwise possible.
Futility of physical life surmounted...
While memories and connections help to
complete,

Driven onto spiritual excellence.
Grief and sorrow bitter;
Yet, resolution sweet.

To thrive,
Rather than survive each moment.
The goal,
Even as tears,
Anguish,

Laughter flows,
Simultaneously.
The wonder of brokenness,
Torn asunder,
Plunged unwillingly,
Into that torrent of a sea.

Such strength,
I've never encountered before.

The Resilience of this eternal soul...
Which enriches,
Inspires,
Me, forevermore!

JLR Spear

Return unto Me

Hunger,
In the pit of stomach,
Though already having eaten.
Feeling useless,
To any but myself this day.
Peace,
Joy,
Relief...
Gone;
Mere memory of yesterday.

I once felt strong,
Loving,
Valiant.
Before weariness,
Taring,
Beating from...
Most the recent assailant.

Rise,
Fall,
Too often.
Would rather stay,
For a time...
Risen.
Having removed traps,
Cage,
Starvation,

Imprisonment.

Usual me vanished,
Vacant page.

Drawn,
Grief stricken,
Too week to stage...
A war to escape.

Hope dim,
Someone,
Retrieve me,
From hole,
I did not dig.
Promise,
Wasn't me who chose,
The state I'm in.

No matter,
Much as I resist,
Ripped by another,
Plucked away,
Bound at wrists.

No permission given,
No invitation,
Unexpected begs and pleas,
From me...

To anyone willing to listen.
Security,
Freedom,
Love,
Peace...
Return unto me,
PLEASE!

JLR Spear

Returned to the Living

Holding the hand,
Of tomorrow...
Gets me through today.
When mistakes,
Breaks,
Disdain are eventually,
Swept away.

Day awakens,
With at least one more chance...
To alter thoughts,
Beliefs,
And more forward,
Advance.

Leaving the past in the past,
Embracing change!

Determined resilient,
Strong,
Solid.
Building upon all,
Previously learned,
Divorcing,
Sad,
Sordid.

Holding greatly,

To a refreshing beginning;
Joy unspeakable,
The day of lingering old...
Ending.

Keeping weary,
Weighted eyes on the good,
Which lay ahead...

Letting the shattered fall away,
Goodbye,
Stench of decay and death.

Filling the nostrils,
With fragrance of blooms,
Letting rains wash all away,
Cleaning and healing wounds.

Begin again,
One step forward,
Shoulders confident and squared.
Being alert,
Alive,
To allow myself to,
Run and share...

The path of another,
Desperate to hear my words...

"Come let us walk together,

On a freshly tilled earth".

Extending newly gained strength,
And lending encouragement,
Imagery,
Hope,
Given...
Lightening as lightened,
Heightened senses,
Preparing...
Inspiring,
Having finally returned...
To the living.

JLR Spear

Shall Not Receive

Give,
Give,
Give,
More required.
Spiritually distanced,
Physically forced,
Into fire.
Needs not met,
Effort,
Effort,
Effort,
Tried.
No one there,
Silent cry.
Sacrifice,

Trust misplaced.
Search for compassion,
Upon any human face.
Broken,
Wounded,
Continually abused.
Retreat,
Rebuild,
Heal...
Left,
Confused.
Humbling self,

Reaching out,
Ask...
Instead,
Given another task.

Hearing others...
Unheard myself...
"What about me?"

Echoed still,
From everyone else.
To be seen,
To be heard,
I'd give anything...
Learning self-love,
Choosing,
To believe.
Finding more,
Often than not...
Ask...
And you shall not,
Receive.

JLR Spear

She Returned

I know the terror,
Heart-wrenching feel,
Of a child missing...
Pleading,
Gasping,
Searching for hours,
Hoping,
Bargaining.

Time standing still,
A dream,
Twilight...
Of thought.
Not a second wasted,
Nor a thought on demise,
Or even being distraught.

Action,
Seeking wisdom,
Tireless treading anywhere,
Instead...
Pushing far from me,
Any doubt,
Or vision of possible death.

Calling,
Driving,
Her last known steps traced,

Remembering her resourcefulness.
Her strength to push and pull through,
Find the way out of the dark woods,
Panicked and alone.
Dreaming…
Believing,
Imagining she would find her way home.

After many, many hours,
That is exactly what she did.
And just like that,
A new candle of faith within her,
Was lit.

Relief,
Tears of fulfilled good.
Peaceful trust within imagination…
Melted into truth…
Actualization.

Not to say,
There were not bad choices,
Many consequences to learn from,
And endure.
All that mattered in the end,
However…
She returned.

JLR Spear

Spectrum Grief

Extreme loss,
Some feel deeper,
Than others...
Even the loss,
Of those not known too well.
Yet depth,
Of anguish,
Darkness,
Tragedy,
Felt.

Some move on,
More easily.
Leaving it behind.
Others,
Continue to love,
Yet constructively,
Are deeper entwined?

Continuing forward,
Yet holding on closer,
Than even before.
Being changed,
Forever enlightened,
And more sensitive,
Than before.

I am the latter,

Though former,
I have tried to be.
However, try as I may,
Only through deep connection,
I'm somehow set free!

Remembering,
Healing,
Embodied with those lost...
Truth.
I've lived this,
Undeniably,
Despite my youth.

I am an old soul,
Trying to bring,
Honor and peace...
To the beautiful,
Yet ill,
Deceased.

JLR Spear

Spiritual, Physical Need

In need,
Moment to moment,
For something,
To touch me...
So deep,
So magnificent,
Tender,
Undeniably.
In discomfort,
Pain,
I reach as far as I am able...
Into the realms,
Praying for something,
Compassionate,
Stable...
That I may rest,
For just a minute,
Torn to shreds.
I need,
I want,
I ache,
Inside...
Body,
Spirit,
With pounding head.
Love given,
Belief,
Shown.

Please,
Bestow to me now...
Comfort unknown.
Undone...
Messy inside and out.
Need,
Want,
Return to me,
Faith,
Overcoming doubt.
Tattered,
Someone...
Give,
As once,
For you,
I did.
Rare,
Truly it is,
To find me,
Bare.
Come,
Soothe,
Parched,
Cracked as I am.
Extend to body,
Love,
Strength giving,
So I may stand.

Just stay here,

As I struggle,
From slumped,
Miserable...
In need,
Of sweet,
Helpful,
Gentle touch,
Spiritual and physical.

JLR Spear

Stand

Leaving much to be repaired,
Yet welcomed relief...
Then comes the surge again,
To cleanse brutally...
All which was rebuilt,
Such is the human life...
A majestic, aging house,
By the ocean on faulty stilts.

To be continuously managed,
And rearranged...
Sustaining through lots of massive storms,
Unplanned...
Yet how can one believe a house built,
Amidst the sea,
Would truly stand.

JLR Spear

Surrendered, Yet Angry

Infuse my heart,
With something,
To hold to...
Tell me it will get better,
Not worse,
As in the past;
It tends to...
Go all wrong,
For months;
Leaving me barely hanging on.
Give me faith,
In action,
A word,
A touch,
A song.
Make the darkness disburse,
With certain heavenly light.

I need a touch,
From the Heavens,
Spiritual,
Insight.
I am more harshly struck,
Than before...
Even with the excruciating trials,
So recently passed.
There's only so much,
One soul can possibly,

Outlast.
I have stood valiantly through,
Three lifetimes of heartache...
There is not one more,
(Though I have said this before)
I can endure.
Still,
I am expected to do so,
Though I have begged,
And pleaded for help...
Doing good in the midst of it all,
Anyway.
Is it truly,
Too much to ask...
For something,
Lasting or good?
That will not be killed,
Snatched away?
My patience is gone,
My insides scream,
Crying out for some relief.
If all I've had to bare,
Given of others,
In anguish and grief.
Here I'll stay,
Here I'll wait...
Not doing one more thing,

Required of me...
Until I am heard,
Answered,
Satisfied and gain something,
Desired.
I am through giving,
Beyond my physical and emotional,
Resources,
Rather out of need.
Not one more thing I'll accomplish,
Until I have rightfully received.

JLR Spear

The Dirge

Lament,
Soul's song,
For her...
Passed.
Those gone before,
Beyond our grasp.
As we weep,
And sing,
The saddest of songs.
They enter unto peace,
And continue on.
Nothing will remove,
The imprint left...
From the souls touched,
Though hearts bereft.
Mourn,
Remember,
Hold the torch close,
Through which she is seen again...
Into one flame converge...
Though hearts cannot contain,
The pain,
Lost,
Though she remains...
Still onward...
The Dirge.

JLR Spear

The Last Dance

The parking lot,
Of a coffee shop,
Police found your body.
In your car,
Shortly after a successful meeting,
With your payroll officer.

You scored and got java,
Then breathed your last.
Needle to the ankle,
Slumped over,
What a way to pass.

Fentanyl found,
In your car,
And in your bloodstream,
Stopped.

I suppose you decided,
That would be your last say...
With the cops.

No more meetings,
No more probation,
Or hearings.
You were a doctor after all...
Humiliated...

You gave yourself to the drug you came
to love.
Last dance,
With your demon,
Deciding,
No longer would you run.

The heights you reached,
Plunged you far beneath...
The lowest you would ever go.

Hiding,
Stealing,
Crawling,
Needing...
Needle's last blow.

Wish you'd found peace,
Somehow been set free...
Of the neurological effects of abuse,
Fentanyl,
Death,
To autopsy.

Maybe it wasn't truly that,
In the end...
Perhaps love lost or the abuse you
received,
Constant disappointments,
Ridicule,

Was what brought you to your knees?

I miss YOU!
The soul you were in flesh,
Without all of it.
You were well,
For a time,
Until this very last slip.

I miss your face,
Expressions,
Your laugh...
The way you'd squint your eyes.
Here I sit now,
Left in all the raw facts,
While you are now free?!...
I am not going to lie...

It kills me,
I am angry,
A part of me selfish...
Saddened you took that chance,
Intentional or not,
Knowing you could end it all,
Did you mean to?
Having given the demon on last dance?

JLR Spear

The Soul's Tourniquet Binds

Moment comes,
In life,
Nothing will do.
Thirst unquenchable,
By even vast, fresh lakes of water.
Old,
Ragged,
Seems the new.

Aventura ceases,
Fears inflamed,
Even the most peaceful mind,
Discovers time of nothing received,
Registered,
Nothing Concocted,
Nothing to design.

Eyes burn,
Bones ache,
Distinguishable fire,
Soul,
Body,
Refuse to respond to,
Any fulfilled desire.

Skin crawls,
Nerves rage,
The relief denied of itch.

Unsettling,
Unravelling of,
Deeply,
Tightly drawn stitch.

Innocent intentions,
Meditations,
Inner growth,
Nothing infiltrates...
The dark night of the soul,
Just time,
Eventually deeming it time,
For another state.

No rhyme,
No reason,
Unknown set time...
Relief,
Release,
Of the soul's tourniquet,
Which binds.

JLR Spear

The Voice of a Loved One

Much can ravage,
And wear down the soul.
Daily struggles,
Many will never know...

Of what you go through.
Against all odds,
You prevail.
Walking silently,
Sometimes in despair,
Trudging along,
The heavy trail.

Only you can walk,
The journey,
All on your own.
Desiring not to,
Weigh others down.
As you pull yourself along...
The path you,
And those closest to you,
Have sown.

Then comes the voice,
Tender, sweet, and kind;
To lift your spirit upward,
And to remind...
They are close,

In prayer and in thought.
Regardless of what you are,
What you have,
And what you have not.

That voice continues,
And raises you from the depths,
You have for so long,
Been from.
Priceless,
Serene...
Comfort finally comes,
In the form of the voice...
Of a loved one.

JLR Spear

Think Twice!

Please, think twice,
Before barreling in with judgement,
And criticism.
You do not know what the other person,
May have experienced that day.
The heart may have been dealt,
Another hard blow,
While you continue to blow it,
It further away.

A look,
A condescending tone,
An outright disregard,
Of words and thoughts...
May have that loved one,
Pushed too far down,
Sadly wrestling,
Feeling distraught.

Check yourself,
Before you enter...
And offer your supposed good advice and
view,
Think of how you would receive;
All of that which you would say,
On a rough day...
If that loved one was you.

JLR Spear

This Can't Be Real

Waking up,
Optimistic for the day,
To begin with fresh
Perspective, a plan.

Within the first 30 minutes,
Upon waking,
I am taken back,
To yesterday again and again.

The battles fought,
And won,
Become an illusion instead.

Swirled speech of sadness,
And hate,
Are hurled my way.

Met with love,
And understanding,
Yet, fear would not allay.

I'd wipe away tears,
Hold her,
Life in survival mode,
Trying to keep,
Her from harm.

Continually searching,
Applying solutions,
Falling short,
With constant alarm.

Well intentioned friends,
Speechless,
Unable to step in
Objectively.
While I run here and there,
At FULL speed,
Spinning wheels...
Perspectively.

So many attempts,
Therapy,
Meds,
With love,
To help heal.

Instead,
A vortex of,
Crushed dreams,
Broken heart,
Feeling of,
This can't be real!!!

JLR Spear

To Those Left Behind

It is astonishing to me,
All a person can mean...
Once they are gone.
Embarrassing,
To say the least.
The need for their presence,
Becomes far stronger.

Then there are questions and regrets,
Of, "why didn't I spend more time with
you?"
Although to them,
In the end,
It doesn't matter...
Their love was and is pure and true.

The past falls away to them,
While the one left,
Holds it closer.
It is you...
Not they,
That seek to find closure.

Their being is with you,
More present and alive...
Nothing manufactured...
No pretense,
Nothing contrived.

Unearned,
Blessing of togetherness,
Closing the great divide.
A true gift,
Bestowed...
All past slights removed.
Hope,
Peace,
Strength,
All that now remains inside,
Of the one set free...
Believing,
Imparting the same,
To those left behind.

JLR Spear

Torturous World

Distraction,
Impossible to ignore,
All pull my attention away.
Increased irritability,
Wanting others to come close,
Then leave...
No... Stay.

Confusion,
Outrage,
Then love and hope,
Changes one moment to the next.
It would be nice to deny,
Yet,
I press on...
Preparing,
Willing myself to accept...
That life will never be,
At least for now,
Any type of normal.
I reach out,
Retreat,
In this low,
Settling grief...
So informal.
Sickening,
Writhing...
To strangely laughing at your words;

Spoken when you were here,
With me,
Feels so absurd.
One day,
I am told...
This too shall pass...
For now,
I live in a torturous world,
Lacking a functional compass.

JLR Spear

Tragedy

The body and mind numb...
When heart-wrenching tragedy hits.
A shock to the system,
Reeling,
Grasping,
To make the pieces fit...
Back into place,
As it was before,
Somehow.
Yet,
Impossible to erase...
The forever changed now,
Ripped from me,
What I adore.

Awakening days later,
Realizing...
The recent event will not dissolve.
The new normal,
In motion...
A whole other puzzle to solve.

Pain,
Anguish,
Fear,
Held back by a dam...
Protecting the system from overload.
Now let loose,

Flooded...
Slammed.

Emotions take over,
No longer holding back at all...
The gravity of so much settles,
As the tears builds to a vast, pounding
waterfall.

Crushingly real,
It wasn't just a dream.
I was inches away from losing you...
Sickening suspense muting the inner
scream.

Prayers of protection,
Instinctual,
Said for days before your disappearance,
Collision, Crash!
So much could have been lost.
You stepped out mostly untouched,
From the ash.

So much feeling now,
Rushes in and hard to contain...
Larger than my entire body.
Much disbelief,
Then relief,
Sadness,
Then anger...

Impossible for all to be embodied.

Releasing,
Letting go,
Still concerned for your future,
As almost the same happened three
months ago.
Just with no wounds to suture.
Beneath the faith,
Support,
Love and unconditional motherly things...
I cannot deny my warnings for you.
I cannot deny my disgust for your
choices,
And the utter fright they bring.
As we all heal from this,
Can only hope for a wakeup call?
Transitions to abundant change,
Transparency...
Awaking to learn the value of life,
Choices we make,
In the wake of and to prevent further,
Tragedy.

JLR Spear

Tragic fall

What more could you have possibly done,
To have kept this from happening?
One side step,
One different word,
You ponder...
One decision made slightly a different
way,
For now, the silence of her absence,
Is deafening.

You know the truth is,
She made her own decisions,
Without your consent or control.
Yet, it doesn't make it easier...
Or make you question loss less,
She will never get the chance to become
what she wanted,
No chance to grow old.

Weren't you supposed to go first...?
Leaving her with much wisdom.
The spirit of her lingers,
Haunts...
As well as her smile.
Her laugh...
Her careless soul;
Winsome.

Many memories,
Many regrets.
As you barely make it through the day,
Intimate with the cycle the grief.
Instead of celebrated successes,
Birthday parties...
You set on the grave with tears...
A commemorative wreath.

The circle of life disrupted,
Sequence upset.
So many pictures,
Still shots in your mind,
Churn,
Ripping your heart,
Leaving you... left.

The seasons will come and go,
No less painful with the years.
Feelings will never be the same.
Though it may not help,
Many others have cried those bitter tears,
You, by far, are not to blame.

Events, choices, free will of others,
Ravaged your once peaceful shore.
This cruel and harsh world left you little
of,
All that existed before.

She left this world,
Knowing how much you loved and cared.
You were held so dear to her,
Though for you..
.

It wasn't enough...
Feeling less than,
Lacking,
Reason blurred.

"How would you know?
How I feel?"
You ask.
"It is I,
Mom"...
I have watched and regretted,
You are sad.

I speak to you,
Aloud,
To prove I exist,
I live,
Just not physically where you are,
Right now.
I am free,
I have moved on,
Just wish you could somehow.

I know you weren't perfect,
Still your heart so good,

Full,
Dedicated,
And strong.
Know that I love you,
I am with you,
Always,
In you through all.
I never wanted this to happen,
I was shocked,
Shaken myself...regretting the tragic fall."

JLR Spear

Wiser Father and Man

The moment I met you...
Light and passion,
Exploded into me.
I believed!
You were the one to finally,
Set this heart bound,
Completely free.

I was enraptured,
Captivated and held.
I could accomplish all things,
Drawing you completely into myself.

As time moved on,
I began to see...
Deep,
Dark,
Harsh restlessness in you.
I began to feel unsettled,
Concerned,
That my very soul was in danger,
Of being consumed.

Soon, sudden violent outbursts,
Frantic fury,
Desperation...
You took advantage,
Of my love,

Trust,
Absolute dedication.

You began to steal light,
From my eyes...
My demeanor.
Taking me far away from,
Those I love.
Even in moments of great loss,
Of my parents, my nephew,
You would demand,
Criticize,
Take me below,
Rather than lift me above.

The answer lay within me,
The love from my daughter's sad,
Confused eyes.
As well as from my sister,
One by one beginning to ask "WHY?"

Why would I endure such treatment?
Isolation,
And abuse?
I have found,
I didn't even notice,
Feeling, perhaps,
I deserved,
Being misused...

My affections,
Time,
Fortune,
Had I not somehow earned,
The disappointment?
I had made my bed,
Should I not lie in it?
I have failed others,
Making poor life choices.

Yet,
In my daughter's eyes,
Reflecting in part,
Mine...
I realized I must leave you know,
Leaving "us" behind.

My sins are forgiven,
I am loved...
Cared for by those who are honest,
Sincere,
Intentions pure.
Though it grieves me,
Tares at my soul...
The answer is sure.

You unlikely will allow,
Me to walk away without the worst,
Of all fights.
Still... I must let go,

And let you fade into the dark night.

Away from me,
Away from those I love,
And whom I must protect now.
I loved you,
With all of me,
I cannot help you find yourself,
I cannot please you anyhow.

I must cut the ties,
I foolishly bound myself with;
Releasing you to wicked ways,
Set adrift.

Secured,
Worthy,
As are all those I love,
Praying protection on such,
From your coming wrath,
I'll no longer be drugged...

Or deceived by false promises,
Of change,
I will...
Drink the elixir of truth,
Toward freedom,
Ingest the bitter pill.

Goodbye to you,

False soul mate...
My presumed salvation.
I will and must save myself,
My daughter,
Forming a new foundation.

As you go,
Know,
I truly loved you with all I had.
Learning so much,
To take along my own path.

One of self-love,
Respect,
Honor and worthiness,
I deserve.
To be loved by me,
Unconditionally,
Becoming self-assured...

Okay in becoming an example,
Of what not to do...
Losing myself to another,
Having denied my own personal truth.

Rebuilding begun,
With this first step...
On the way to who I truly am.
Better than what you made me,
Or took from me,

I'll now stand...
As an overcoming,
Protecting,
Wiser father,
Wiser man.

JLR Spear

You Do Not Walk Alone

A young lady walks in the wood,
Among the canopy of trees.
Breathing in the fresh air,
Provided,
Strolling among stones,
Grass,
Falling leaves.

Her heart is heavy,
Burdened by present and past.
Searching for the meaning of it all...
Beyond the looking glass.

Rays of the sun,
Peak through,
The limbs swaying above.
She walks along,
Taking in the lush surroundings,
Yet feeling less than good enough.

A nearby stream,
Trickles and flows,
Providing a smooth,
Sweet, bubbling voice.
Muted,
Pleasant music,
Her soul creates,
Soothing,

Releasing,
Lingering mental noise.

Quietly she moves onward,
Now feeling a strange comfort...
Somehow a welcoming touch?
She is unaware...
It is a beloved friend,
Just lost to death...
Lovingly hovering,
In the brush...
Wishing her well,
Sending her love,
Forwarding appreciation,
Of all they've shared.
Unseen to this girls',
Physical eyes...
Another dear,
Soul is there.

Strolling along,
Behind her,
Unhindered,
Is her recently,
Old four-legged companion.
Lost to old age.
Now out of pain,
She hasn't left her abandoned.
Gleefully,
The renewed pup follows,

As she has for years.
Yet, now without,
Aching hips...
Wishing to once more,
Allay best friend's fear.

Calm and gently,
There's warmth,
All around this wanting,
Searching girl.
Her precious,
Wondrous,
Friends accompany her,
Though no longer,
A part of this physical world.

Beneath,
The heartache,
Endless grief.
She's lightened,
For a moment,
With great kindness...
Emanating from friends,
Tree canopies, and streams.

The girl stops,
Listens,
Looks around.
Flooded with peace,
As if she is truly home...

Though she may not see...
She feels,
Quiet,
Still...and hears a whisper...
"You do not walk alone."

JLR Spear

Your Soul's Projection

It saddens my soul,
You won't truly understand,
Or really get to know me,
Until you remove the film...
From your eyes...
Remove walls built up...
So, I will set myself,
Free.

I am me,
You are you,
I hope one day,
You examine inwardly,
And produce...
The ability to love,
Others unconditionally,
Becoming accepting and loving,
Especially to yourself.

Choosing to look inward,
Attempting not to judge.
Finding what you truly seek,
When others speak...
Projections of themselves?

I understand,
I have been there...
Felt the need to erect structures for
safety,
And run for cover...
It is all a mental form of protection.
Still until the film is removed from eyes,
Walls come down,
You will not heal.
I remain the wall to you...
Upon which will show only your soul's
projection.

JLR Spear

Zephyr

The season of tragedy,
Illness,
Death...
Has come and gone.
Now ushering in,
A new time of life,
Blessing,
Peace,
Plenty,
And songs...

Of love,
All needs and desires,
Mostly met...
Forgiveness,
Release,
A time to forget.

No matter the state of a broken nation,
As repair for it,
Possibly arising soon...
Now,
This family's time of Harvest,
Reward,
Enjoyment...ensues.

Darkness to Light,
Sickness to health,

Weakness to strength.
Showers to sunshine,
Spreading through height,
Depths,
Widths, and lengths.

Moving onward,
Forward,
A new glorious path created...

With goodness,
Truth,
Special,
Being separated...

From the woes and trials,
That were fought.
With continual vision,
Will prosper now,
In magnificent images and thoughts.

No holding back now,
Run,
Dance,
Explore...
Yes, some grief will always stay,
To which I will back up,
At times... to rest,
Heal,

The recurrent sore.

Remaining hopeful,
Imaginative,
Artistic,
Secure and assured.
Feeling at times I am grasping,
At straws...
Still vapors,
Sediments,
Enlightenment...
Saturate,
Best permeating all.

Rejecting thoughts,
Words,
Deeds of less,
And ignorance...
Repelling lies,
Disasters,
Far from imminent.

Due to the healing,
Protection,
Covering... of the more powerful,
Enjoyable streams,
Running throughout,
Will be without obstacles,

The subconscious river...
Flowing free.

Life giving water,
Quenches,
The demonstrative drought that swept
through...
Wind of change,
Gentle and sweet,
Takes ours spirits to the NEW!

JLR Spear

About the Author

JLR Spear...letters representing various loved ones crossed over as well as part of the name of the author sharing all inspired, experienced, shared with through others' experiences, writing it all in raw, poetic form...
A collective, collided, voice, soul, mind, spirit of individuals living as well as honoring those crossed over. God's hand, heart, love, benevolence extended to all humans who remain and those to come in future.
JLR Spear is a conduit through which encouragment, compassion, peace, kindness, consideration, and creativity flow to humans open and ready to receive. This conduit is an expression of many
stories as well as having experience much itself. Not of just male, female, white, black, asian, indian, rather all blended into one, is JLR Spear. Without prejudice, without judgement, a creative source to give and share. Child-like yet alive in this earthly shell for an appropriate amount of time to have wisdom, insight, and understanding. Anonymous and willing

to speak to all humans for all humans and that of past, present, and future subjects of spiritual and physical subjects, important to many. JLR Spear wishes to make a difference with life-sharing, life-giving impact upon the spirits housed within the bodies present now, and future. JLR Spear is also, the child lost at birth and even before birth, one lost in the early years, teen and young adults, and adults lost to suicide, accidents, murder, drug addiction, diseased, and those lost to natural causes late in life. The spirit lives on eternally.

Residing in the heavenlies, as we all do through meditational prayer, mostly, alive and well here on earth for now...and will continue long after this shell is gone, so is JLR Spear. Inspirator of receptive people to believe in themselves, do the self-work, reach beyond, create, discover... and death is never final, never the end of existance, rather just the beginning.

What will your now, future, eternity be? Only you can create it. You are that powerful!

Blessings and honor to you...

NAMASTE- I bow to you, Sanskrit

VEDE, PATS, SALAM, LAPE', HACANA, MIR, SANTI, ZHI-BDE, PAU,

MINAGGEN, DOHIYI, HEDDWCH, FRED, FRIEDE, IRINI, PCO, PAZ, BAKE',
SOLH, PAIX, SIOCHAIN, SHEE, SANTI, UDU, FRIDIUR, HEIWA, RONGO, VREDE, POKOJ, MIR, PACE, SANTIPAP, SHALOM, BARIS,
Peace be with you in 35 different languages.

~JLR Spear

www.ingramcontent.com/pod-product-compliance
Lightning Source LLC
Chambersburg PA
CBHW072224150726
48002CB00005B/1942